Disability 4 A Day

Therapist's Handbook

Michelle McFalls-Mills, OTD, OTR

Balboa Press books may be ordered through booksellers or by contacting:

Balboa Press
A Division of Hay House
1663 Liberty Drive
Bloomington, IN 47403
www.balboapress.com
1-(877) 407-4847

Because of the dynamic nature of the Internet, any web addresses or links contained in this book may have changed since publication and may no longer be valid. The views expressed in this work are solely those of the author and do not necessarily reflect the views of the publisher, and the publisher hereby disclaims any responsibility for them.

The author of this book does not dispense medical advice or prescribe the use of any technique as a form of treatment for physical, emotional, or medical problems without the advice of a physician, either directly or indirectly. The intent of the author is only to offer information of a general nature to help you in your quest for emotional and spiritual well-being. In the event you use any of the information in this book for yourself, which is your constitutional right, the author and the publisher assume no responsibility for your actions.

Certain stock imagery © Thinkstock.
Any people depicted in stock imagery provided by Thinkstock are models,
and such images are being used for illustrative purposes only.

ISBN: 978-1-4525-5980-3 (e)
ISBN: 978-1-4525-5979-7 (sc)

Library of Congress Control Number: 2013910949

Printed in the United States of America

Balboa Press rev. date: 08/29/2013

Table of Contents

Introduction

As I matured as an occupational therapist, I learned that my mission to help those in need changed. Not only would I continue to serve those with disabilities as a therapist, but also to serve the communities in which my clients worked and lived. The service I needed to render to those without disabilities was to counter those common misconceptions about the disabled, to build sensitivity, to educate and to counter negative attitudes that would often border on bigotry or ignorance that could lead to harm.

My approach was to ask those without disabilities to 'walk in another's shoes', and to be 'disabled for a day.' It is the effective way I have found to build respect and empathy toward those with disabilities. I have watched people change their perspective from seeing only disabilities, to seeing a disabled individual as a whole person, as human and varied as anyone else.

My fond hope is that you will find this program will make you witnesses to this remarkable transformation in attitude and perception.

Sincerely,

Dr. Michelle McFalls-Mills, OTR/L

Acknowledgments

I would like to thank my Mom, Dad, Joyce and Wendy for always supporting me in all my life endeavors and believing in me. Thank you to all of my friends and coworkers for your encouragement and inspiration. Thank you to Dr. Patricia Slocum for taking time to mentor and support me during the publishing process. If it were not for you, I would not be completing the publishing process and having the opportunity to share my program. Thank you to the Occupational Therapy Department at Creighton University in Omaha, Nebraska. Your continued support and encouragement helped to make the program what it is today. I would also like to thank North Thurston Public Schools' administrators and staff in Lacey, Washington for allowing me to implement The Disability 4 A Day Program and conduct my research project in Seven Oaks and South Bay Elementary Schools. Your openness, understanding and support of my program are and always will be greatly appreciated.

Vision Statement

Our goal is to work with school staff, parents, 1st grade thru college-aged students, community members, coworkers, and family members to increase awareness and empathy for individuals with disabilities, promote the occupational therapy and other rehabilitation professions, and increase the knowledge of the human body through role-play and discussion.

Mission Statement

Disability 4 A Day is a one-day, hands-on experience that will enhance the perspectives of school staff, students, and community members about those with disabilities, while promoting occupational therapy and other rehabilitation professions and educating participants about the human body.

Program Description

The Disability 4 A Day program has been developed to be implemented in one school building one classroom at a time, or a working facility one department or daily shift at a time. It was originally designed to be implemented during April, Occupational Therapy Month, but it can be implemented year round. Each participating classroom or department is assigned one full day. In schools, the day of participation is determined by the program therapist and/or the classroom teacher. In a working facility, the participation day is determined by the program therapist, whether it be an Occupational Therapy (OT), Speech/Language Pathology (SLP), or Physical Therapy (PT) professional, and the department supervisor.

When implemented in the school building, other participants, such as parents and other school staff, are welcome to participate in the program as well. The day of parent and staff participation is determined by the program therapist and the participating adult.

Timeline

The program timeline is based on activities selected by the classroom teacher or department supervisor and the program therapist. (For Set-up procedures, please see Get Started section on page 30.)

The following timeline is based on one elementary school building's schedule. **Please change it according to your school's schedule and to what activities are selected by the classroom teacher.**

The following is a sample program schedule for an elementary school whose day begins at 9:00am, ends at 3:20pm, includes all optional activities and has an occupational therapist as a program leader.

9:00am Enter participating classroom. When class is ready, begin summary of the occupational therapy profession.

9:10am Explain program rules. Answer any questions that may arise about the process. Once everything has been explained, begin the program.

9:20am Assign disabilities to volunteers and begin taping.

LUNCH During the classroom's lunch time, check in and see how things are going and re-tape where needed or required. After lunch, the program continues.

2:45pm Hold class discussion with visiting friend, a student or an adult with a physical disability, complete experience hand-out and teacher feedback forms, and human body quiz.

3:20pm Program ends.

The following is a sample program schedule for a working facility whose day starts at 7:30am and ends at 6:00pm, includes group discussion and experience forms as the selected activities, and has a physical therapist as the program therapist.

7:30am Department or shift members meet to discuss the program with the program therapist. Deliver a brief introduction to the therapist's discipline if participants are interested.

7:40am Explain the program rules and procedures. Answer any questions. Once all questions and/or concerns are attended to, begin the program.

7:50am Assign disabilities to participants and begin taping.

LUNCH Check on participants and address any questions and concerns. Re-tape if needed. 5:00pm Hold a department discussion on disability experience and complete experience forms. 5:55pm Program ends.

Program Rules

These rules are very important for maintaining proper safety and to facilitate learning from the program.

- REMEMBER—the program is voluntary. All students or employees do NOT have to participate.
- Take the disability seriously.
- If the involved body part starts to hurt, loses circulation, or experiences pain in any way, remove tape and dispense in garbage.
- If the participant wants to remove the disability before the end of the day, remove tape and dispense in garbage, take off clip and return index card to program therapist or remove yourself from the wheelchair and return to program therapist.
- If the participant gets frustrated, stop the disability and return program items to the program therapist.
- The visually-impaired participants require a reliable assistant to guide him/her through school or work facility environment, during lunch time and through certain desk tasks.
- At the end of the day, please return glasses, identifications cards (index cards with disability written on them) and wheelchair to the program therapist before leaving the classroom or work facility. If you had a disability that required tape, please remove tape and dispense in the garbage or place in backpack or work bag to share the experience with family, friends, or coworkers.
- NO switching disabilities after they have been assigned.
- The most important rules of all are to HAVE FUN and LEARN from this experience.
- The wheelchair participants are required to follow the rules above as well as the following:
    - Do not purposely run into people.
    - Do not use the wheelchair as a toy.
    - When using the restroom, you may remove yourself from the wheelchair. If you are interested in trying to transfer yourself from the wheelchair to the toilet, please discuss with the program therapist for transfer technique and transfer with caution. If at any time you feel you may fall or tip over, please remove yourself from the wheelchair immediately and use the restroom as you usually do.
    - When stationary (at desk, in classroom, or in hallway), LOCK BRAKES.
    - Attempt to negotiate the doors of the building. If you require assistance, ask.
    - Other students, school staff, coworkers, or adults may not assist unless asked.

Why Masking Tape?

The reason to utilize masking tape to create the "disability" is because of the thinness of the tape which makes it easy for the participant, teacher, other school staff member, or adults to tear and remove.

If a participant feels pain, appears to lose circulation of the involved body part, or becomes frustrated, he/she can tear the tape off easily without assistance.

If the child or adult has an "affected" arm, where the arm is taped to the body, the individual continues to have the freedom for proper reaction reflexes if he/she stumbles to protect themselves against injury.

Disabilities List

The following are the recommended disabilities for this program. The bolded words are to be written on the index cards for identification purposes. The number of index cards used for each disability depends on supply availability (wheelchairs, glasses, etc.) and the program therapist's personal preference.

Arm — Choice

Figure 1.0

- **Arm (choice)**: The arm of the participant's choice is taped to his/her body to simulate a unilateral (one side) disability (see figure 1.0).

Arm — Dominant

Figure 1.1

- **Arm (dominant)**: The dominant arm of the participant is taped to his/her body to simulate a unilateral disability (see figure 1.1).

Arm — Non-Dominant

Figure 1.2

- **Arm (non-dominant)**: The non-dominant arm of the participant is taped to his/her body to simulate a unilateral disability (see figure 1.2).

Blind

Figure 1.3

- **Blind**: The eyes/vision of the participant are entirely blocked by tape-covered sunglasses to simulate a visual disability (see figure 1.3).

Eyes Bilateral

Figure 1.4

- **Eyes (bilateral)**: The eyes of the participant are blocked by tape-covered glasses that allow vision through a small hole on each side, simulating a visual disability (see figure 1.4).

Eyes Unilateral

Figure 1.5

- **Eyes (unilateral)**: The eyes of the participant are blocked by tape-covered sunglasses that allows vision through a small hole on one side of the glasses (see figure 1.5). Which side of the taped glasses have the hole is determined by the program therapist.

Hand — Choice

Figure 1.6

- **Hand (choice):** The hand of the participant's choice is taped, with the thumb in the adduction position, to simulate a unilateral disability (see figure 1.6).

Hand — Dominant

Figure 1.7

- **Hand (dominant):** The dominant hand of the participant is taped, with the thumb in the adduction position, to simulate a unilateral disability (see figure 1.7).

Hand — Non-Dominant

Figure 1.8

- **Hand (non-dominant):** The non-dominant hand of the participant is taped with the thumb in the adduction position, to simulate a unilateral disability (see figure 1.8).

Non-Verbal

Figure 1.9

- **Nonverbal:** Participant is unable to utilize words to communicate, simulating a communication disability (see figure 1.9). Participant can laugh, scream, grunt, etc. They are unable to form words.

Thumb — Choice

Figure 1.10

- **Thumb (choice):** The thumb of the participant's choice is taped in adduction position next to the index finger to simulate a coordination and opposition disability (see figure 1.10).

Thumb — Dominant

Figure 1.11

- **Thumb (dominant):** The thumb of the participant's dominant hand is taped in adduction position next to the index finger to simulate a coordination and opposition disability (see figure 1.11).

Thumb — Non- Dominant

Figure 1.12

- **Thumb (non-dominant):** The thumb of the participant's non-dominant hand is taped in the adduction position next to the index finger to simulate a coordination and opposition disability (see figure 1.12).

W/C

Figure 1.13

- **W/C (wheelchair):** The participant is assigned to remain in the wheelchair for the duration of the day, or for as long as the participant can handle, to simulate a severe lower extremity physical disability (see figure 1.13).

Yes/No

Figure 1.14

- **Yes/No:** Participant is able to communicate verbally to others utilizing only the words "yes" and "no", simulating a communication disability (see figure 1.14).

Disabilities Taping Techniques

Please note that participant safety is the number one priority. Do not tape tightly around involved body parts. Please make sure that the involved body parts are taped loosely. <u>If you select a different disability than those listed in this handbook, tape at your own risk.</u>

Arm

1. First, wrap the selected arm with paper towel or other protective material—enough to cover all exposed skin.
2. Next, have the participant rest the selected arm on the abdominal region and wrap fingers around his/her side so the elbow is at a 90° angle and the entire arm is against the body (see figure 2.0).
3. Have the participant raise the opposite arm, enough so you can wrap tape around the axillary/trunk area to help with stabilizing the affected arm.
4. Wrap a few straps of tape around the humerus of the affected arm up to the axillary area of the raised arm—enough to stabilize the arm against the trunk as well as to give it room to move slightly (see letter a in figure 2.0).
5. Bring the raised arm down and keep to the side.
6. Wrap a few straps around the forearm and wrist to assist with keeping the protective material on the arm.
7. Wrap a strap of tape around the forearm from near the elbow crease to the upper trapezius of the same side as the affected arm (see letter b in figure 2.0).

8. Finally, wrap tape around wrist and guide the strap to the upper trapezius of the opposite side, and bringing it around to place the end on the affected forearm (see letter c in figure 2.0).

Please note that figure and tape will change depending on the dominant or non-dominant arm. If you feel additional tape is required for stability and safety, please add at your discretion.

Figure 2.0

Blind

Retrieve the glasses or sunglasses that are being used for the program. Tear pieces of tape in pieces approximately 14 inches in length. Place tape on hard surface with the sticky side up. Open the frames of the glasses and place one of the sides on the middle of the tape—start in the middle of one of the ear frames. Once the glasses are in the middle of the tape, bring the top portion of the tape end in and place on the inside of the ear frame so the top half of the tape is now bent and the sticky sides are stuck together (see figure 2.1).

Take the end of the bottom portion and bring it to the ear frame (see figure 2.2). Once the first piece is in place, tear another piece of tape and place on it on a hard surface. Repeat the previous instructions. It is very important to make sure the tape pieces stick to the piece next to them. This forms a sturdy blinder. Continue with the instructions until you get to the middle of the opposite ear frame. Once all tape is in place, check to see where additional pieces may need to be placed for extra support. Cut out a nose area. You may need to place tape along the inside of the nose space so there are no sharp pieces from the scissors. After the nose space is made, measure at least 2 inches from the bottom of the glasses to the bottom portion of the tape blinders on both sides. After measuring the 2 inches on both sides, draw a line to connect the two measurement and you have a continuous line that is approximately 2 inches wide. Repeat to the top portion. Cut the lines on both portions. After you have cut on the line, you should have 2-inch-wide tape blinders that cover the entire pair of glasses (see figure 2.3 and 2.4).

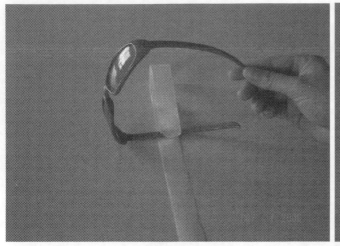

Figure 2.1

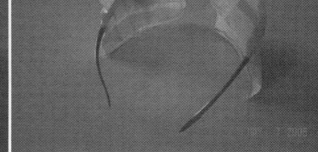

Figure 2.2

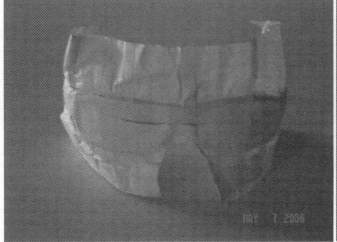

Figure 2.3

Figure 2.4

Eyes (bilateral)

Follow the same taping procedure as the blind glasses. The only change to this pair of glasses is to make sure and leave holes on both sides of the glasses, enough that some vision is still possible. The size of the holes can vary depending on your personal preferences.

Eyes (unilateral)

Follow the same taping procedure as the blind glasses. The only change is to this pair of glasses is to make sure and leave only one hole on one side of the glasses, enough that some vision is still possible. The size and side of the hole can vary depending on your preference

Hand

1. Have the participant retrieve enough paper towel/protective material to cover all skin on the hand.
2. Have the participant supinate the "affected" hand and place the thumb in the adduction position (see letter A in figure 2.5).
3. Wrap the paper towel/protective material around the hand to cover all skin (see letter B in figure 2.5).
4. Wrap tape around the hand until most of the paper towel/protective material is covered with the tape (see letter C in figure 2.5).
5. Continue until the hand is covered (see figure 2.5).

Please note that taping will change depending on dominant or non-dominant hand.

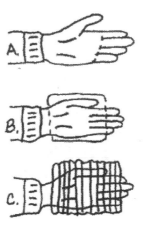

Figure 2.5

Nonverbal

This disability does not require any tape. The only requirement is to clip the card onto the participant with the badge adapters so his/her peers, friends, or coworkers are aware that they are experiencing a communication disability.

Thumb

1. Have the participant fetch sheets of paper towel/protective material—enough to cover the skin around their thumb and palm area of the hand.
2. Have the participant supinate the affected hand and place the thumb in adduction position (see letter A in figure 2.6).
3. Wrap paper towel/protective material around the thumb and the palm area of the thumb (see letter B of figure 2.6). Do not block or tape over the MC-P joints as this is a thumb disability not the hand.

4. Wrap tape around the thumb and palm so the thumb is comfortable and difficult to access (see letter C of figure 2.6).

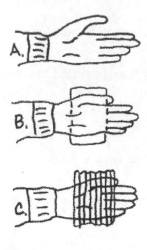

Figure 2.6

Wheelchair

No tape is required for this disability. Have the participant sit in the wheelchair and make sure it is a safe size. It is recommended that the participants who are to experience wheelchairs are placed in chairs that are the proper size and fit. If the participant is too big or too little for the wheelchair, please have him/her select a more appropriate card.

Yes/No

No tape is required for this disability. The only requirement is to clip the card to the participant with the badge adapter so his/her peers, friends, or coworkers are aware that the participant is experiencing a communication disability.

Supplies

Required

As you begin getting things together to start the program, do not forget to include the following items, or similar items, as they are required for completing the program.

- **Badge adapters**: These are used to clip the disability cards to the participating person—to inform others of his/her disability when the participant might not be able to; i.e., have a communication "disability". The disabilities that require badge adapters include: blind, eyes (bilateral), eyes (unilateral), yes/ no, and nonverbal.
- **Index cards**: These are utilized for disability identification. The disabilities are written on the index card. Each participant selects a card, which are facing down. The card that is selected is the disability which the participant will be simulating for the day. Laminating these cards, if you have a laminator available, after the disability is written on them, protects them from tearing and ripping during the program. Laminating will increase the longevity of the index cards.
- **Masking Tape**: Masking tape is utilized as the cohesive part of the disabilities and assists with the visual disabilities. It stabilizes the "disabled" body part by holding it close to the body to decrease the chance of injury and decreases the use of the involved body part during the disability experience. It also blocks vision through the sunglasses for the visual disabilities.
- **Permanent marker**: The marker is utilized to write the disabilities on the index cards. Using pen and pencil, at times, is difficult to read as they are not dark enough and can smear.
- **Sunglasses**: The glasses are used for the visual disabilities. It is recommended to purchase inexpensive sunglasses as you may use multiple pairs throughout the program implementation.
- **Wheelchair**: The wheelchair is used for a severe, lower extremity physical disability. The participant remains in wheelchair for the duration of the day.
- **Paper towels or other protective material**: The paper towel/protective material is used as a barrier to the skin. It protects the skin from acquiring an injury or skin reaction due to the masking tape.

The amount needed for each of the above items will depend on the number of participants in the program and access to quantity of each supply item; i.e., wheelchair, badge adapters, etc.

Optional

These items are separated into three categories:

- **Promotional**: These items are used to promote the program therapist's profession. Possible examples: pencils, key chains, and stress balls, all depending on your interest and budget.

- **Participating**: These items are given to the program participants as a thank you. Possible examples range from small items like pencils, candy, and erasers to big items like bags, shirts, and notebooks, all depending on your interest and budget.
- **Prizes**: These items are given to the winners of the human body quiz. You may have one prize for both questions or one prize per question.

These items are optional. You can decide whether you want to include them in your program. Please remember to select items that are safe and appropriate for school-aged children when implementing the program in a school building.

Handouts and Forms

This program requires several handouts and forms. Do not worry, I will describe the forms and explain the purpose for each of them. After reading about and understanding the forms, you may decide not to use all of them in your program. **However, it is highly recommended that all appropriate forms and handouts are used.** The forms and handouts are all located in the Appendices in the back of this handbook.

Introductory Packet (IP)

The first five handouts and forms are given as an <u>Introductory Packet</u> (IP) to all classroom teachers or staff members of the participating department. The packet can also be given to parents and other school or business staff, if requested. The main reason for the IP is to introduce and familiarize staff or parents with the program and the program therapist's profession. The packet also allows the recipients to demonstrate their interest in participating in the program. For the work facility introductory packet, the "Why is Occupational Therapy in Schools?" form is not needed. If the program therapist is of a different discipline (i.e. a speech or physical therapy), please feel free to include literature regarding that profession as well. The Introductory Packet includes the following:

Disability 4 a Day (tri-fold) (Appendix A)

This is an informative handout that allows the reader to learn about the program. It includes a short description of the program, its vision, and mission statements, as well as testimonials. [Please note that the pamphlet is a two-sided sheet that should be folded in a tri-fold manner.]

What is Occupational Therapy? (Appendix B)

This handout allows teachers, school staff, coworkers, or community members to read a general overview of the occupational therapy profession, the settings that occupational therapists are qualified to work in and ultimate goals of occupational therapy. *If the program therapist's profession is different than OT, please include information about profession with the IP if interested.

Why is Occupational Therapy in School? (Appendix C)

This handout should only be included in the IP for a school. This handout answers the question that many teachers and school staff may have about occupational therapy in the school environment. It allows them to read and become familiar with the purpose of school-based occupational therapy. Basically, it explains why occupational therapy staff do what they do in school buildings.

*If the program therapist's profession is different than OT, please include information about profession in the school setting with the IP if interested.

Program Description (Appendix D)

This handout describes the program. It explains the activities that are available within the program. Along with activity descriptions, the interest form instructions and the program's therapist's contact information are made available. (See figures 3.0 and 3.1).

If you are interested in participating or having your classroom or department participate in this learning experience, please complete the interest form and place it <u>in my mailbox.</u> I will contact you with more information so we can begin planning your participation date and activities. Please read through the other handouts that are included in your packet.

Figure 3.0

If you have any questions, comments, or concerns, please contact me at <u>(123) 456-7890 x1234</u> or via email <u>ot@myschool.k12.wa.us.</u>

Figure 3.1

Interest Form (Appendixes E & F & G)

These interest forms are given to the teacher, parent, or staff member to complete. They will inform the program therapist of three things: first, if they are interested in participating; second, what program activities they would like to partake in; and, finally, on what dates they are available to participate. The bottom of this form includes a signature line for consent and the contact information of the program therapist. ***If the program therapist is not interested in implementing any of the program's activities, i.e. human body quiz, "N/A" should be written on the line in front of that activity on the interest form so teachers, parents/guardians, staff members, or coworkers will be unable to check it as an area of interest. The program therapist's contact information should be written on the forms prior to the distribution of the packets. (see figures 3.2, 3.3, and 3.4).**

Teacher Interest Form

School:_____ Grade:_____

Teacher's Name:_____

Please check the appropriate Disability 4 a Day areas below in which you would like your classroom to participate:

_____ Yes, I am interested in participating in the Disability 4 a Day program.

     I am interested in the following activities:
     _____ Description of the Profession of _____
          therapy
     _____ My classroom participating in the disability experience
     _____ A classroom discussion on the disability experience
     _____ Classroom completing an experience worksheet
     _____ Participating in the human body quiz

     I am interested in participating on one of the following dates:
     _____
          (Please circle all dates that apply.)

_____ No, I am not interested in participating in the Disability 4 a Day program.

_____ _____
Teacher's Signature   Date

Thank you for taking the time to complete this form. If you volunteered your classroom to participate, a letter containing your classroom's participation date and a letter to send home to inform parents/guardians of the program will be placed in your mailbox soon. If you have any questions, please contact me using the information below. Thank you, again, for your interest in the Disability 4 a Day program.

_____ _____
Program Coordinator   Contact Information

Appendix E

Figure 3.2

Staff Interest Form

Work Facility:_____ Department:_____

Staff Member's Name:_____

The Disability 4 a Day program leader _____, is interested in implementing the following activities on the date of _____. Please check the areas in which you are interested in participating. If the activity has "N/A" on the line in front of it, this activity is not included in the program schedule.

_____ Yes, I am interested in participating in the Disability 4 a Day program.

     I am interested in the following activities:
     _____ Description of the Profession of _____
          therapy
     _____ Participating in the disability experience
     _____ Dept/Staff discussion on the disability experience
     _____ Completing an experience worksheet
     _____ Participating in the human body quiz

     I am interested in participating on one of the following dates:
     _____
          (Please circle all dates that apply.)

_____ No, I am not interested in participating in the Disability 4 a Day program.

_____ _____
Staff Member's Signature   Date

Thank you for taking the time to complete this form. If you have any questions, please feel free to contact me. Again, thank you for your interest in the Disability 4 a Day program.

_____ _____
Program Coordinator   Contact Information

Figure 3.3

Parent/Guardian/School Staff Interest Form

School:_____ Grade:_____

Name:_____
Please Circle One: Parent/Guardian School Staff _____
                           Contact Information

Please check the appropriate Disability 4 a Day areas below in which you would like to participate.

_____ Yes, I am interested in participating in the Disability 4 a Day program.

     I am interested in the following activities:
     _____ Description of the Profession of _____
          therapy
     _____ My classroom participating in the disability experience
     _____ A classroom discussion on the disability experience
     _____ Classroom completing an experience worksheet
     _____ Participating in the human body quiz

     I am interested in participating on one of the following dates:
     _____
          (Please circle all dates that apply.)

_____ No, I am not interested in participating in the Disability 4 a Day program.

_____ _____
Participant's Signature   Date

Thank you for taking the time to complete this form. If you have any questions, please feel free to contact me. Again, thank you for your interest in the Disability 4 a Day program.

_____ _____
Program Coordinator   Contact Information

Appendix G

Figure 3.4

The top portion of the form is for the classroom teacher, parent, or staff member to complete. The middle section of the form is for the interested party to complete to indicate either interest or noninterest in participating in the program. If interested, the activities are listed for the participant to check. The blank line at the bottom of the middle section is for the interested party's signature.

*The program therapist is required to list the available dates and his/her contact information before distributing IP (see figures 3.5 and 3.6).

I am interested in participating on one of the following dates:
April 3, 4, 5, 6, 7,   17, 18, 19, 20, 21   24, 25, 26, 27, 28.
(Please circle all dates that apply.)

Figure. 3.5

Thank you for taking the time to complete this form. If you have any questions, please feel free to contact me. Again, thank you for your interest in the Disability 4 a Day program.

Holly Misner, OTR/L
Program Coordinator

(347) 275-1398 x437
Contact Information

Figure. 3.6

Other Forms

Parent/Guardian Letter (Appendix H)

The parent/guardian letter is given to each participating classroom student to take home to inform his/her parents/guardians about the program and the student's chance to participate. All teachers should send copies of this letter home three or more days prior to their classroom participation date. This allows the parents/guardians time to contact the teacher, program therapist, or the principal with any concerns, comments, and/or questions about the program (see figure 3.7).

Parent/Guardian Letter

Date:_____, 20_____

To: Parents/Guardians of_____'s Class

Re: The Disability 4 a Day program

Dear Parents/Guardians:

Good day. My name is_____and I am the _____ therapist at ____ _____ School. As you can see from the statement above, I will be implementing a program in hopes to increase the awareness of____therapy and empathy toward individuals with disabilities through the Dis abilit y 4 a Day program. The individuals who volunteer to participate in the program will be given a physical disability. For example, a student who selects the card with "blind" on it will be given glasses to block their vision or a student who selects dominant arm will have their dominant arm taped to their body to simulate a muscular disability. At the end of the day, all students in the classroom, whether they participated, assisted, or observed, will take part in a class discussion of their disability experience. An overview of the program is below:

- One classroom will be participating a day
- The participating classrooms are volunteered by their teacher
- At_____am, the classroom will be given a description of the profession of _____therapy.
- After the introduction, participating students will be given their disability.
- The students will participate in normal school activities with their disability.
- Around_____pm, the classroom will have a discussion to share their experiences and observations.

Please note that your child does not have to participate in the program. It is on a volunteer basis. Your student's teacher will be given the date when their classroom will be participating. **The program is also open to parents/guardians as well.** If you are interested in participating in the program or have questions or concerns regarding the program, please contact me using the information below. Thanks and have a good day. ☺

Appendix H

Sincerely,

_____
_____
_____
Work: _____
Email: _____

Appendix H

Figure 3.7

When you are ready to complete and copy the parent/guardian letter, be sure to fill in all needed information before making copies. Remember: each classroom receives separate letters. Enter the date, the teacher's name, the program therapist's name, and the school where the program is being implemented (see figure 3.8). Lastly, complete the contact information, and print and sign your name (see figure 3.9).

Date:_____March 15_____, 20 11

To: Parents/Guardians of_____Mrs. Smith_____'s Class

Re: The Disability 4 a Day program

Dear Parents/Guardians:

Good day. My name is_____Craig Thor_____and I am the _____Physical Therapist at_____East Elementary_____School.

Figure 3.8

20

Sincerely,

Craig Thor, PT

Work: (815) 235-0114

Email: cthor@myschool.com

Figure. 3.9

Confirmation Forms (Appendix I & J & K)

This form is given to the teacher, parent/guardian, or staff member to inform them of the date they or their class will be participating in the program. The date selected is one of the dates that the teacher, parent/guardian, staff member, or program therapist designated on the interest form. This form is utilized as a reminder and it also provides a deadline for finalizing all details and answering any questions (see figure 3.10, 3.11 and 3.12).

Teacher Confirmation Form

Date:_____, 20_____

To: _____

Re: Confirming interest in and participation date for Disability 4 a Day program

Dear Teacher:

Thank you for your interest in participating in the Disability 4 a Day program. This letter is confirming your interest in the program and, based on the dates you selected on the Teacher Interest Form, your participation date is:

_____, 20_____

The activities you selected on the interest form are the activities that will be completed on the date above.

I am interested in meeting with you for 5 minutes the day before your participation date to go over the details of the program and address any questions or concerns you may have. If you would like to meet at a different time, please contact me so we can change it at_____or via email at_____. Again, thank you for participating in the Disability 4 a Day program.

Sincerely,
_____
_____
Work: _____
Email: _____

Appendix I

Figure 3.10

Staff Member Confirmation Form

Date:_____, 20_____

To: _____

Re: Confirming interest in and participation date for Disability 4 a Day program

Dear_____:

Thank you for your interest in participating in the Disability 4 a Day program. This letter is confirming your interest in the program and based on the form you completed on the Staff Member Interest Form, your participation date is:

_____, 20_____

The activities you selected on the interest form are the activities that will be completed on the date above.

Thank you for participating in the Disability 4 a Day program. If you have any questions, please do not hesitate to contact me using the information below.

Sincerely,
_____
_____
Work: _____
Email: _____

Appendix J

Figure 3.11

Figure 3.12

Confirmation forms require some information be filled in prior to delivery. You will need to write the date that you are completing the form and address it to the appropriate person (see figure 3.12).

Date:_____ March 30 _____, 20 11 _____

To:_____ Mr. Jones _____

Figure 3.13

Now fill in the date that you selected for the participant and your contact information on the lines provided (see figure 3.14).

_____ April 18 _____, 20 _11_

The activities you selected on the interest form are the activities that will be completed on the date above.

I am interested in meeting with you for 5 minutes the day before your participation date to go over the details of the program and address any questions or concerns you may have. If you would like to meet at a different time, please contact me so we can change it at _____ (815) 235-0114 _____ or via email at _____ cthor@myschool.com _____

Figure 3.14

Lastly, print your name and school or company/department title and sign the form (see figure 3.15).

Again, thank you for participating in the Disability 4 a Day program.

Sincerely,
_____ _Craig Thor, PT_ _____
_____ Physical Therapist _____
_____ East Elementary School _____
Work: (815) 235-0114
Email: cthor@myschool.com

Figure 3.15

Feedback Form (Appendix L)

This form is given to all teachers who volunteer to have their class participate and/or to all adult participants. This form collects feedback on program areas that may need improvement as well as noting things that are done well.

Participant Experience Form (Appendix M & N & O)

This form allows participants—both students and adults—to write about their experience. The form includes an area to compare the ways his/her day was similar or different with a disability. It also includes an area to state whether he/she did or did not enjoy their experience and whether he/she would participate again. The form allows for great feedback and for discovering where the participants had a difficult time or enjoyed themselves and what they learned. There are three different participant experience forms: one for 1st through 4th grade students, one for 5th through 12th grade students, and one for adults.

23

Human Body Quiz (Appendix P)

The human body quiz forms are available if the organizer opts to include the quiz in the program. These forms are a fun way to quiz what participants know about their bodies and to learn about it while having fun. Each sheet has two separate questions. The answers to the questions are located in the back of the handbook. If the program includes the quiz, prizes are optional and are not required.

The quiz forms are not in any specific order. Please choose questions that are age appropriate (see figure 3.16).

Do not forget to cut and separate quiz forms before distributing them!

Human Body Quiz	Human Body Quiz
Name:_____ Teacher:_____ Is the tongue a muscle? _____ How many vertebrae are there in the spine? _____	Name:_____ Teacher:_____ Is the tongue a muscle? _____ How many vertebrae are there in the spine? _____
Human Body Quiz	Human Body Quiz
Name:_____ Teacher:_____ Is the tongue a muscle? _____ How many vertebrae are there in the spine? _____	Name:_____ Teacher:_____ Is the tongue a muscle? _____ How many vertebrae are there in the spine? _____

Figure 3.16

Supply List Price Inventory Form (Appendix Q)

This form is a two page form that allows you to inventory the required and optional supplies as well as calculate the cost of your program with a clear and easy to follow format.

Please note: the financial aspect of this program can range greatly, depending on the amount the program therapist determines as a financial limit.

The more employer furnished items are utilized the less the total cost of the program. Purchasing multiple optional supplies will increase the program cost. Either way the program can be successful.

The overall amount is determined by the program therapist.

Begin the first page of this form by listing the required supplies, the package size, and the price of the package (see figure 3.17).

Required Supplies		
Item	Package size (dz/lb)	Price of Package
Badge adapters	dz	$2.00
Index cards	100 cards	$5.00
Masking tape	Roll	$2.00
Permanent marker	2 pack	$3.00
Glasses	Single	$1.00
Wheelchair	Single	
Paper towel	Roll	$1.00

Figure. 3.17

For the items that will be furnished by your employer, there is no need to complete the package size and price. Simply mark the employer furnished column. If your employer will not furnish the supply, complete all columns. This entire process allows you a better idea of the financial needs of your program.

Please note that you may need to estimate on some quantities required or wait until the interest forms are turned in for a final count.

When you are ready to complete the rest of the form, fill in the last five columns of each supply item and calculate the total for quantity purchased and the program cost column. The required supplies cost is labeled (A) and will be required later to determine the total cost of your program. (see figure 3.18).

Quantity Purchased	Total Cost	Program Purchase	Employer Furnished	TOTAL PROGRAM COST
3	$6.00	X		$6.00
1	$5.00		X	-----
10	$20.00		X	-----
1	$3.00		X	-----
10	$10.00	X		$10.00
			X	-----
3	$3.00		X	-----
			Total A	$16.00

Figure. 3.18

25

If you are not including any optional supplies in your program, "A" is your total program cost.

If you are offering optional supplies, begin page 2 of the Supply List Price Inventory form by following the same process as page 1. Begin by listing the supplies under the proper category as you did on page 1 (see figure 3.17).

Promotional Supplies		
Item	Package size (dz/lb)	Price of Package
Pencils-April-Occupational Therapy Month	dz	$3.00
Participation Supplies		
Item	Package size (dz/lb)	Price of Package
Pencils-OT mth-Disability 4 a Day	dz	$3.00
Prize Supplies		
Item	Package size (dz/lb)	Price of Package
Bone pens	dz	$5.00
Interlocking Puzzle Candy Skel etons	dz	$15.00

Figure 3.19

The supply list in figure 3.19 includes pencils (personalized with "April—Occupational Therapy Month") for promotional purposes, pencils (personalized with "Occupational Therapy Month—Disability 4 a Day") for participants, and bone pens and interlocking puzzle candy skeletons for the human body quiz prizes. When you are ready, complete the rest of page 2 (see figure 3.20).

Quantity Purchased	Total Cost	Program Purchase	Employer Furnished	TOTAL PROGRAM COST
25	$75.00	X		$75.00
			Total B	$75.00
Quantity Purchased	**Total Cost**	**Program Purchase**	**Employer Furnished**	**TOTAL PROGRAM COST**
25	$75.00	X		$75.00
			Total C	$75.00
Quantity Purchased	**Total Cost**	**Program Purchase**	**Employer Furnished**	**TOTAL PROGRAM COST**
3	$15.00	X		$15.00
3	$45.00	X		$45.00
			Total D	$60.00
		Page 2		

Figure. 3.20

After completing page 2, place the dollar amounts that are labeled "A", "B", "C", and "D" on page 2 in the corresponding areas on page 1 (see figure 3.21).

Add Total B:	+ $75.00
Add Total C:	+ $75.00
Add Total D:	+ $60.00
PROGRAM GRAND TOTAL:	=
Page 1	

Figure. 3.21

Add "A", "B", "C", and "D" to find the total cost of the program. Figures 3.22 and 3.23 show fully completed forms for reference (see figures 3.22 and 3.23).

Supply List Price Inventory Form

Required Supplies							
Item	Package size (dz/ lb)	Price of Package	Quantity Purchased	Total Cost	Program Purchase	Employer Furnished	TOTAL PROGRAM COST
Badge adapters	dz	$2.00	3	$6.00	X		$6.00
Index cards	100 cards	$5.00	1	$5.00		X	-----
Masking tape	roll	$2.00	10	$20.00		X	-----
Permanent marker	2 pack	$3.00	1	$3.00		x	-----
Sunglasses	1	$1.00	10	$10.00	X		$10.00
Wheel-chair	Single					X	-----
Paper towels	roll	$1.00	3	$3.00		X	-----
						Total A	$16.00

Totals		
Add Total A:	+ $16.00	
Add Total B:	+ $75.00	
Add Total C:	+ $75.00	
Add Total D:	+ $60.00	
PROGRAM GRAND TOTAL:	=$226.00	

Figure. 3.22

Promotional Supplies							
Item	Package size (dz/lb)	Price of Package	Quantity Purchased	Total Cost	Program Purchase	Employer Furnished	TOTAL PROGRAM COST
Pencils-April-	dz	$3.00	25	$75.00	X		$75.00
Occupational							
Therapy Month							
						Total B	$75.00

Participation Supplies							
Item	Package size (dz/lb)	Price of Package	Quantity Purchased	Total Cost	Program Purchase	Employer Furnished	TOTAL PROGRAM COST
Pencils-OT Month-	dz	$3.00	25	$75.00	X		$75.00
Disability 4 a Day							
						Total C	$75.00

Prize Supplies							
Item	Package size (dz/lb)	Price of Package	Quantity Purchased	Total Cost	Program Purchase	Employer Furnished	TOTAL PROGRAM COST
Bone Pens	dz	$5.00	3	$15.00	X		$15.00
Interlocking Puzzle	dz	$15.00	3	$45.00	X		$45.00
Candy Skeletons							
						Total D	$60.00

Figure. 3.23

Quick Reference and Mini Rules Sheet (Appendix R)

This brief list provides rules that are very important for maintaining proper participant safety and to facilitate learning from the program.

Get started

Okay. It is time to get started. The following is the recommended step-by-step process. It can be changed according to your preferences.

1. First, and most importantly, make sure that you **want** to complete the program. This program requires extra time and energy to implement.
2. When implementing the program in a school environment, discuss the program with your school principal and special education director, or in a work environment, discuss the program with the department supervisor. It is important to verify support of you and the program. If a parent, coworker, or other supervisor has concerns he/she may contact the supervisor, who will be capable of answering any questions or concerns relating to the program.
3. Write a list of the required supplies and verify availability.
4. Complete a Supply List Inventory form. Take note of needed supplies and the funding amount required to complete the program.
5. After completing the Supply List Inventory form, analyze information and decide if you or your department is financially able to implement the program.
6. Complete the Program Description handout and fill in your contact information.
7. In the Teacher or Staff Member Interest form, fill in the optional dates.
8. Make enough copies of the handouts and forms of the Information Packet (IP) to give to all school (1st thru 12th grade) or college teachers/professors, coworkers, or staff members, and place one in the staff lounge for other staff to read, whether in a school or work setting. Collate the IP handouts and forms and distribute them to school or working staff, either placing them in their mailbox or placing the packet on their desk.
9. While waiting for the interest forms to be returned, complete the disability cards (see the supplies section on page 14). Prepare the sunglasses for the visual disabilities.
10. As interest forms are returned, place each form in a community folder for safe keeping. Begin to schedule classrooms, school staff, parents, and staff members for participation depending on the days requested by teachers and the program therapist's schedule.
11. Complete and distribute the confirmation form for all teachers, parents, and staff members.
12. Complete parent letters for participating classes. Make sure to give the letters to the teachers to send home with students several days prior to the participation date.
13. Check to make sure all supplies are available and start the first program participation date.

Opening Day!

For the opening day, pack supplies and place them near the participating classroom/department (tape, paper towels, wheelchairs, disability cards, and taped glasses).

When the bell rings or work day begins, enter the classroom/department and wait for students/staff to be seated. Depending on the activities selected by the teacher or program therapist, the day may start with an Occupational Therapy (or other discipline) introduction or the teacher/therapist may dive straight into distribution of disabilities and taping.

a. **Therapy introduction**: Make sure that any explanation is grade level appropriate and in laymen terms. Please try to limit the summary to 2-5 minutes to keep participants' attention. Then continue to the distribution of disabilities and taping.

b. **Distribution of disabilities and taping**: Ask student and adult volunteers to line up in single file near you. Remember it is on a volunteer basis. Mix up disability cards and place them face down. One person at a time selects a card and returns to his/her seat. You may be asked if the participants are allowed to switch or exchange disabilities. It is not recommended. The reason being that individuals who live with disabilities are unable to choose their disabilities.

c. Preparation for the various disabilities should be as follows (the categories can be called in any order). Calling each disability individually will assist with crowding:

d. **Arm**: Ask those who have index cards that have "arm" written on it to retrieve some sheets of paper towel/protective material—enough to wrap all exposed skin around the entire arm. If the student/adult has a long-sleeved shirt, paper towels are not required because the shirt protects the skin from the tape. Tape the assigned arms using the proper taping technique. When all arms are complete, call another category (for example, "vision").

e. **Vision**: Hand out glasses to students according to their assigned vision disability. At this time, announce that those with visual disabilities, especially the blind, will require a reliable, assistant. It is recommended that the teacher/supervisor assigns the helpers as they will know who may be a good assistant. When all glasses and assistants are assigned, call another category (for example, "hand").

f. **Hand**: Ask those who drew "hand" to fetch enough protective material to wrap around all ex- posed skin of the entire hand. Tape the assigned hand using the proper taping technique. When all hands are complete, call another category (for example, "nonverbal").

g. **Nonverbal**: Explain what nonverbal means and discuss other means of communication the nonverbal students/participants can use throughout the day. Clip the nonverbal cards onto the students/adults. The nonverbal day begins as soon as the card is clipped onto their shirt. When all nonverbal cards are distributed, call another category (for example, "thumb").

h. **Thumb**: Ask those who drew "thumb" to fetch enough protective material to wrap around their thumb and hand. Tape the assigned thumb/hand using the proper taping technique. When taping thumbs, please tape for continued access of the MC-P joints of the fingers as it is only the thumb the participant is not to use. When all thumbs are complete, call another category (for example, "yes/no".)

i. **Yes/No**: Explain what "yes/no" entails and clip the card onto participants' shirt. The yes/no day begins as soon as the card is clipped onto their shirt. When all yes/no participants are complete, call the last category (in this example, "wheelchair").

j. **Wheelchair**: Ask the students/adults who have chosen the wheelchair card to come and select a chair. Please make sure that the participant's size is a proper fit for the wheelchair that he/she will be in for the day. After all students/adults are in their chairs and the entire class—including the teacher/supervisor—is listening, explain the wheelchair rules.

After all disabilities have been prepared, explain the program rules and the importance of following the rules.

At lunch or break time, take this opportunity to check on the tape and make adjustments if needed. Also, ask to see if anyone has any questions or concerns at this time.

Wrap up

The end of the day is the wrap up session. This session consists of the activities selected by the classroom teacher and/or program therapist. The activities may include group discussion, completing an experience form, completing a feedback form, and the administration of the human body quiz. You may also take this time to bring in a friend—a student or an adult living with a disability—to join the class, especially for the discussion.

Class/department discussion: You may have many questions that you would like to ask. If not, here are some ideas. Please state questions in an age appropriate manner:

- How was your day or experience?
- Was there anything that was hard or difficult during your disability experience?
- Was there anything that was the same or unchanged during your disability experience?
- Was anyone stared at?
- Did anyone get picked on or made fun of? If yes, how did that make you feel?
- What did you learn today?
- Are all disabilities physical or noticeable to others just by looking at a person? Discuss "inside" or internal disabilities – ADHD, Autism, Learning Disability, etc.

The discussion time span depends on how many wrap-up activities were selected as well as the preference of the program therapist. If additional activities were selected, it is recommended to keep the discussion/visitor question time around 10–20 minutes. However, every program is different and the time of the discussion can vary depending on the program therapist's schedule.

If an individual with a disability is joining the discussion group, introduce him/her at the beginning of the discussion so they are involved as well. I have found the discussion to be especially meaningful when including an individual with a disability. Giving participants the opportunity to learn about daily struggles and successes first hand opens their eyes and minds. Encouraging them to discuss and share their experience with their peers increases the impact of the discussion so that awareness, respect, and empathy grow and become contagious. *If there are inappropriate questions or comments, it is recommended to stop the questions or comments and move on.*

Participant Experience Forms and the Program Feedback Form: If the time is plentiful, distribute the participant experience form for the students/adults to complete. While the participants are completing the experience forms, ask the teacher/supervisor to complete the feedback form. If there is a shortage of time, the Program Feedback form and Participant Feedback form can be given to the classroom teacher/staff members to fill out at a later time.

Human Body Quiz: After the forms have been completed or given to the teacher/supervising therapist to complete at a later time, hand out the human body quiz. Please select age appropriate questions. You can use a different quiz form for each classroom/department, depending on the number of participating classes/departments. This will assure that the participants do not have the chance to share answers. It is recommended that you allow at least two minutes for the participants to write down their answers or guess and turn in the sheet. As the quiz forms are being returned, separate the correct or close answer sheets from the others. It saves time to be able to announce the winners after all the forms are turned in instead of having the participants wait for you to look and find the winners. If you have many that have correct or close answers, place them face down and have the teacher/supervisor select the number of names that correlates with the number of prizes.

After the quiz is complete, thank them for participating and, if you opted to include a promotional and participation item, pass them out at this time. Describe what each item is for and let them know why they are receiving it. After all is complete, ask if there are any questions. If there are no questions, thank them again. *Please include a statement regarding future interactions with ALL individuals, especially those with disabilities, in school, at work, or in the community. Ask the participants to remember their "disability 4 a day" experience during these interactions, and how it felt to walk in someone else's shoes for a day; to experience the struggles and successes for one day that someone with a disability faces every day. Ask them to remember that individuals with disabilities do not have the choice to "stop" their disability when it gets hard or when someone makes fun of them and that they deserve the same respect that we expect. Will the interaction be different or more inspiring than before participating in this program?

After all participating classes, staff, and parents/guardians have completed the program and returned all feedback forms, it is recommended that the program therapist read through all participant experience and feedback forms to gain insight on what aspect of the program went smoothly and what areas may need improvement. It is up to the program therapist to make needed changes!

What I learned about my disability experience is it's what's on the inside of a person that counts.

Rebecca, 8 years old

What I liked most about my disability experience is everything.

Kris, 7 years old

What I liked most about my disability experience is I could feel however people feel with a disability.

Daniel, 9 years old

Here are two ways my life was different with a disability. The first way, I could just wash one hand. The second way, I could only read with one hand holding the book. There are many ways my life was the same with a disability. One example, I could walk. Another example, I could also talk. As you can see, my life with a broken arm was hard and fun.

Alissa, 7 years old

DISABILITY
4 A DAY
PROGRAM

Walk a Day in Someone Else's Shoes
Michelle McFalls-Mills, OTD, OTR/L

Program Description

The Disability 4 a Day (D4AD) program incorporates role-playing and group discussion to increase understanding and awareness of individuals with disabilities. It has been developed to be implemented in one school building, one classroom at a time, or a working facility one department or daily shift at a time. Each participating classroom or department is assigned one full day with participants receiving a physical disability to experience throughout a school or work day. At the conclusion of the day, participants, non-participants, and observers share their experience in a group discussion. It is available to all occupational, speech, and physical therapy staff to implement in a school, work, or community setting.

Vision Statement

Our goal is to work with school staff, parents, 1st grade thru college-aged students, community members, coworkers, and family members to increase awareness and empathy for individuals with disabilities, promote the occupational therapy and other rehabilitation professions, and increase the knowledge of the human body through role-play and discussion.

Mission Statement

Disability 4 a Day is a one-day, hands-on experience that will enhance the perspectives of school staff, students, and community members about those with disabilities, while promoting occupational therapy and other rehabilitation professions and educating participants about the human body.

What is Occupational Therapy?

Occupational therapy is a profession dedicated to helping people achieve well-being through occupation. The term "occupation" represents the flow of activities that fill a person's life and has an effect on his or her health. Occupational therapy is particularly concerned with how people construct meaningful lives individually and in the community.

In the view of occupational therapy, well-being is achieved through an active, dynamic, and evolving balance between the person and his or her environment. Occupational therapists intervene when illness, disability, or social constraints threaten the person's ability to actively create or find balance. Because occupational therapy views people as multidimensional beings, it blends knowledge from the biological and social sciences into a unique, distinct, and holistic profession. In order to use occupations strategically, occupational therapists have expertise in how the body, mind, and spirit work together to produce occupations as simple as feeding oneself or as complex as leading a hundred-piece orchestra.

Occupational therapists help individuals develop, recover, or maintain daily living and work skills of all types. Clients of occupational therapy can be of any age, from newborn infants to the elderly. Sometimes the focus may be on improvement of basic motor functions or reasoning abilities. At other times, living or work environments may need to be modified (Creighton University, n.d.). A wide variety of people can benefit from occupational therapy, including those with:

- Work-related injuries including lower back problems or repetitive stress injuries
- Limitations following a stroke or heart attack
- Arthritis, multiple sclerosis, or other serious chronic conditions
- Birth injuries, learning problems or developmental disabilities
- Mental health or behavioral problems including Alzheimer's, schizophrenia, and post-traumatic stress
- Problems with substance use or eating disorders
- Burns, spinal cord injuries or amputations
- Broken bones or other injuries from falls, sport injuries, or accidents
- Vision or cognitive problems (American Occupational Therapy Association [AOTA], n.d.)

Regardless of type of client or need, the goals for intervention ultimately are to help clients participate as fully as possible in society (Creighton University, n.d.).

American Occupational Therapy Association [AOTA]. (n.d.) Occupational Therapy. Retrieved on March 14, 2006, from the American Occupational Therapy Association Web site: http://www.aota.org/Consumers/WhatisOT.aspx

Creighton University. (n.d.). Occupational Therapy. Retrieved March 21, 2006, from http://spah0.creighton.edu

Why is Occupational Therapy in School?

The act of playing is an important tool that influences a child's life. The primary goals of childhood are to grow, learn, and play. It is often through play that children learn to make sense of the world around them. It is a child's "job" or "occupation" to play in order to develop physical coordination, emotional maturity, social skills to interact with other children, and self-confidence to try new experiences and explore new environments.

School-based occupational therapy is designed to enhance the student's ability fully to access and be successful in the learning environment. Occupational therapists have expertise in evaluating children's neurological, muscular, and emotional development, and determining the effects of infant and childhood illness on growth and development (American Occupational Therapy Association [AOTA], n.d.).

This might include working on handwriting or fine motor skills so the child can complete written assignments, helping the child organize himself or herself in the environment (including work space in and around their desk), working with teachers to modify the classroom and/or adapt learning materials to facilitate successful participation.

In schools, the focus of occupational therapy is on the child's ability to function in the educational environment.

American Occupational Therapy Association [AOTA]. (n.d.) Occupational Therapy. Retrieved on March 14, 2006, from the American Occupational Therapy Association Web site: http://www.aota.org/Consumers/WhatisOT.aspx

Program Description

Disability 4 a Day is a program designed to promote_____therapy, increase the knowledge of the human body through role play and group discussion, and above all increase awareness and empathy in school staff, 1st through 12th grade and college aged students, parents, and community members for individuals with disabilities.

The program consists of several fun and educational activities. The activities include a description of the_____therapy profession, participation in a physical disability experience, a group discussion, and a human body quiz. All activities are optional and are selected by the classroom teacher or program therapist.

The physical disability experience is a volunteer-based program. Physical disabilities will be issued to the participants to experience throughout the school or work day. At the end of the day, all classroom students and staff members, whether they participated or not, will partake in a group discussion to share their experience with their peers. A human body quiz may follow. The quiz consists of two questions about the human body. Each group will have two winners, one for each question. The winners will receive a prize. **Please note that the quiz and the prizes are optional and are decided on by the program coordinator.**

Along with the program description sheet, you have a teacher/staff member interest form. If you are interested in participating or having your classroom or department participate in this learning experience, please complete the interest form and place it_____. I will contact you with more information so we can begin planning your participation date and activities. Please read through the other handouts that are included in your packet. If you have any questions, comments, or concerns, please contact me at_____or via email at_____.

Thank you for your support and interest in Disability 4 a Day.

Teacher Interest Form

School:_____   Grade:_____

Teacher's Name:_____

Please check the appropriate Disability 4 a Day areas below in which you would like your classroom to participate:

_____ Yes, I am interested in participating in the Disability 4 a Day program.

I am interested in the following activities:
_____ Description of the Profession of_____therapy
_____ My classroom participating in the disability experience
_____ A classroom discussion on the disability experience
_____ Classroom completing an experience worksheet
_____ Participating in the human body quiz

I am interested in participating on one of the following dates:

_____

(Please circle all dates that apply.)

_____ No, I am not interested in participating in the Disability 4 a Day program.

_____   _____
Teacher's Signature   Date

Thank you for taking the time to complete this form. If you volunteered your classroom to participate, a letter containing your classroom's participation date and a letter to send home to inform parents/guardians of the program will be placed in your mailbox soon. If you have any questions, please contact me using the information below. Thank you, again, for your interest in the Disability 4 a Day program.

_____   _____
Program Coordinator   Contact Information

Staff Interest Form

Work Facility:_____ Department:_____

Staff Member's Name:_____

The Disability 4 a Day program leader,_____, is interested in implementing the following activities on the date of_____. Please check the areas in which you are interested in participating. If the activity has "N/A" on the line in front of it, this activity is not included in the program schedule.

_____Yes, I am interested in participating in the Disability 4 a Day program.

I am interested in the following activities:
_____ Description of the Profession of_____therapy
_____ Participating in the disability experience
_____ Dept/Staff discussion on the disability experience
_____ Completing an experience worksheet
_____ Participating in the human body quiz

I am interested in participating on one of the following dates:
_____
(Please circle all dates that apply.)

_____No, I am not interested in participating in the Disability 4 a Day program.

_____   _____
Staff Member's Signature   Date

Thank you for taking the time to complete this form. If you have any questions, please feel free to contact me. Again, thank you for your interest in the Disability 4 a Day program.

_____   _____
Program Coordinator   Contact Information

Parent/Guardian/School Staff Interest Form

School:_____ Grade:_____

Name:_____

Please Circle One: Parent/Guardian   School Staff   _____

Contact Information

Please check the appropriate Disability 4 A Day areas below in which you would like to participate.

_____ Yes, I am interested in participating in the Disability 4 a Day program.

I am interested in the following activities:
_____ Description of the Profession of_____therapy
_____ My classroom participating in the disability experience
_____ A classroom discussion on the disability experience
_____ Classroom completing an experience worksheet
_____ Participating in the human body quiz

I am interested in participating on one of the following dates:
_____

(Please circle all dates that apply.)

_____ No, I am not interested in participating in the Disability 4 A Day program.

_____   _____
Participant's Signature   Date

Thank you for taking the time to complete this form. If you have any questions, please feel free to contact me. Again, thank you for your interest in the Disability 4 A Day program.

_____   _____
Program Coordinator   Contact Information

Parent/Guardian Letter

Date:_____, 20_____

To: Parents/Guardians of_____'s Class

Re: The Disability 4 A Day program

Dear Parents/Guardians:

Good day. My name is _____ and I am the _____therapist at_____School. As you can see from the statement above, I will be implementing a program in hopes to increase the awareness of_____therapy and empathy toward individuals with disabilities through the Disability 4 A Day program. The individuals who volunteer to participate in the program will be given a physical disability. For example, a student who selects the card with "blind" on it will be given glasses to block their vision or a student who selects dominant arm will have their dominant arm taped to their body to simulate a muscular disability. At the end of the day, all students in the classroom, whether they participated, assisted, or observed, will take part in a class discussion of their disability experience. An overview of the program is below:

- One classroom will be participating a day
- The participating classrooms are volunteered by their teacher
- At _____ am, the classroom will be given a description of the profession of _____therapy.
- After the introduction, participating students will be given their disability.
- The students will participate in normal school activities with their disability.
- Around_____pm, the classroom will have a discussion to share their experiences and observations.

Please note that your child does not have to participate in the program. It is on a volunteer basis. Your student's teacher will be given the date when their classroom will be participating. **The program is also open to parents/guardians as well.** If you are interested in participating in the program or have questions or concerns regarding the program, please contact me using the information below. Thanks and have a good day. :)
Sincerely,

_____
_____
_____
Work: _____
Email: _____

Teacher Confirmation Form

Date:_____, 20_____

To: _____

Re: Confirming interest in and participation date for Disability 4 A Day program Dear

Teacher:

Thank you for your interest in participating in the Disability 4 A Day program. This letter is confirming your interest in the program and, based on the dates you selected on the Teacher Interest Form, your participation date is:

_____, **20_____**

The activities you selected on the interest form are the activities that will be completed on the date above.

I am interested in meeting with you for 5 minutes the day before your participation date to go over the details of the program and address any questions or concerns you may have. If you would like to meet at a different time, please contact me so we can change it at _____or via email at_____.

Again, thank you for participating in the Disability 4 A Day program.

Sincerely,

_____
_____
_____

Work: _____
Email: _____

Staff Member Confirmation Form

Date:_____, 20_____

To: _____

Re: Confirming interest in and participation date for Disability 4 A Day

program Dear_____:

Thank you for your interest in participating in the Disability 4 A Day program. This letter is confirming your interest in the program and based on the form you completed on the Staff Member Interest Form, your participation date is:

_____, 20____

The activities you selected on the interest form are the activities that will be completed on the date above.

Thank you for participating in the Disability 4 A Day program. If you have any questions, please do not hesitate to contact me using the information below.

Sincerely,

_____
_____
_____
Work: _____
Email: _____

Parent/Guardian/Staff Confirmation Form

Date:_____, 20_____

To: _____

Re: Confirming interest in and participation date for Disability 4 A Day program Dear

Parent/Guardian:

Thank you for your interest in participating in the Disability 4 Day program. This letter is confirming your interest in the program and, based on the dates you selected on the Parent/Guardian/Staff Interest Form, your participation date is:

_____, **20____**

The activities you selected on the interest form are the activities that will be completed on the date above.

I am interested in talking with you before your participation date to go over the details of the program and address any questions or concerns you may have. Please contact me at your earliest convenience at_____or via email at _____ _____. Again, thank you for participating in the Disability 4 A Day

program.

Sincerely,

_____

_____

_____

Work: _____

Email: _____

Feedback Form

Did you enjoy participating in the program?   Yes   No

What activities did you participate in? Please check all that apply.

_____ Description of_____Therapy

_____ Disability experience

_____ Classroom discussion on the disability experience

_____ Complete an experience worksheet

_____ Human body quiz

What was your favorite part of the program?_____

_____

What do you feel may improve the **Disability 4 A Day** program? _____

_____

Would you participate in this program again?   Yes   No

    If no, please state why: _____

_____

How would you rate the D4AD program overall? _____

_____

(Circle one)   Excellent   Good   Poor

Comments: _____

_____

Thank you for your feedback and participating in the **Disability 4 A Day** program!

Disability 4 A Day Program
School Participant Experience Form • 1st – 4th Grades

School _____   Grade _____

Participant's Name _____

Teacher's Name _____

Please complete the sentences below with your thoughts and feelings about your experience.

My 'disability' was _____.

My school day was different in many ways because of my 'disability'. One way was _____

_____

Another way was _____

_____

_____

My school day was the same in many ways even though I had a 'disability'. One way was

_____

_____

_____

Another way was _____

_____

_____

Was your experience fun?   YES   NO

What did you like most about your experience? _____

_____

_____

Would you participate again? (Circle one)   YES   NO

Experience A Day In Someone Else's Shoes

Disability 4 A Day Program

School Participant Experience Form • 5th – 12th Grades

School _____   Grade _____

Participant's name _____

Teacher's name _____

Please complete the sentences below with your thoughts and feelings about your experience.

My 'disability" was _____.

I found the most challenging thing when participating with the disability was _____

_____

_____

The most rewarding part of my disability experience was _____

_____

Did you enjoy your experience? (Circle one)   Yes   No

Would you participate again? (Circle one)   Yes   No

Was your experience fun? (Circle one)   Yes   No

What did you like most about your experience?

_____

_____

_____

Experience A Day in Someone Else's Shoes

Disability 4 A Day Program
Adult Participant Experience Form

Facility/Department _____

Participant's Name _____ Date participated _____

Program coordinator's Name _____

Please complete the sentences below with your thoughts and feelings about your experience.

My "disability' was _____

I found the most challenging thing when participating with the disability was _____

_____

_____

The most rewarding part of my disability experience was _____

_____

_____

_____

Did you enjoy your experience? (Circle one)   Yes   No

Would you participate again? (Circle one)   Yes   No

Comments (regarding specific activities, disabilities, etc. you would like to see as part of the Disability 4 a Day program or any other ideas, opinions, etc.) _____

_____

_____

Human Body Quiz

The following pages offer forms for the administration of the Human Body Quiz. There are two questions on each form, and three forms on each page. These pages can be copied by the teacher or program therapist, cut into three forms, separated, and handed out.

After the appendices of forms, all answers to the quiz are provided.

Human Body Quiz

Name:_____Teacher:_____

How many bones are in the human body? _____

How many muscles are in the human body? _____

Human Body Quiz

Name:_____Teacher:_____

How many bones are in the human body? _____

How many muscles are in the human body? _____

Human Body Quiz

Name:_____Teacher:_____

How many bones are in the human body? _____

How many muscles are in the human body? _____

Human Body Quiz

Name:_____Teacher:_____

How much blood is there in the body? (Please circle one)

        2 quarts   4 quarts   6 quarts   8 quarts

How many bones are in the skull? _____

Human Body Quiz

Name:_____Teacher:_____

How much blood is there in the body? (Please circle one)

        2 quarts   4 quarts   6 quarts   8 quarts

How many bones are in the skull? _____

Human Body Quiz

Name:_____Teacher:_____

How much blood is there in the body? (Please circle one)

        2 quarts   4 quarts   6 quarts   8 quarts

How many bones are in the skull? _____

Human Body Quiz

Name:_____ Teacher:_____

How many bones are there from the knee to the ankle? _____

How many bones are there from the elbow to the wrist? _____

Human Body Quiz

Name:_____ Teacher:_____

How many bones are there from the knee to the ankle? _____

How many bones are there from the elbow to the wrist? _____

Human Body Quiz

Name:_____ Teacher:_____

How many bones are there from the knee to the ankle? _____

How many bones are there from the elbow to the wrist? _____

Human Body Quiz

Name:_____Teacher:_____

    Is the tongue a muscle? _____

    How many vertebrae are there in the spine? _____

Human Body Quiz

Name:_____Teacher:_____

    Is the tongue a muscle? _____

    How many vertebrae are there in the spine? _____

Human Body Quiz

Name:_____Teacher:_____

    Is the tongue a muscle? _____

    How many vertebrae are there in the spine? _____

Human Body Quiz

Name:_____Teacher:_____

    How many ribs are there in the human body? _____

    What do they do? _____

Human Body Quiz

Name:_____Teacher:_____

    How many ribs are there in the human body? _____

    What do they do? _____

Human Body Quiz

Name:_____Teacher:_____

    How many ribs are there in the human body? _____

    What do they do? _____

Human Body Quiz

Name:_____ Teacher:_____

How many bones are there in one hand? _____

How many bones are there in one foot? _____

Human Body Quiz

Name:_____ Teacher:_____

How many bones are there in one hand? _____

How many bones are there in one foot? _____

Human Body Quiz

Name:_____ Teacher:_____

How many bones are there in one hand? _____

How many bones are there in one foot? _____

Human Body Quiz

Name:_____Teacher:_____

    Where is the esophagus located? _____

    What does it do? _____

Human Body Quiz

Name:_____Teacher:_____

    Where is the esophagus located? _____

    What does it do? _____

Human Body Quiz

Name:_____Teacher:_____

    Where is the esophagus located? _____

    What does it do? _____

Human Body Quiz

Name:_____Teacher:_____

How many teeth are there in the adult human body? _____

What are the five senses? _____

Human Body Quiz

Name:_____Teacher:_____

How many teeth are there in the adult human body? _____

What are the five senses? _____

Human Body Quiz

Name:_____Teacher:_____

How many teeth are there in the adult human body? _____

What are the five senses? _____

Human Body Quiz

Name:_____Teacher:_____

    Where is the heart located? _____

    What does it do? _____

Human Body Quiz

Name:_____Teacher:_____

    Where is the heart located? _____

    What does it do? _____

Human Body Quiz

Name:_____Teacher:_____

    Where is the heart located? _____

    What does it do? _____

Human Body Quiz

Name:_____Teacher:_____

    Where are the lungs located? _____

    What do they do? _____

Human Body Quiz

Name:_____Teacher:_____

    Where are the lungs located? _____

    What do they do? _____

Human Body Quiz

Name:_____Teacher:_____

    Where are the lungs located? _____

    What do they do? _____

Answers to Human Body Quiz

The following are the answers to the quiz questions. However, most students will not know and will guess the answer. Please take that into consideration when determining winners. It is up to the program therapist to distinguish the guesses to the winners.

How many bones are in the human body? **206.** How many muscles are in the human body? **630.**

How much blood is there in the body? **6 quarts.** How many bones are there in the skull? **22.**

How many bones are there from the knee to the ankle? **2.** How many bones are there from the elbow to the wrist? **2.**

Is the tongue a muscle? **Yes.** How many vertebrae are there in the spine? **33.**

How many ribs are there in the human body? **24—12 on each side.** What do they do? **They form a protective cage around the heart and lungs.**

How many bones are there in one hand? **27.** How many bones are there in one foot? **26 (28 if you include the sesamoid bones at the base of the big toe).**

Where is the esophagus located? **Neck or throat.** What does it do? **The esophagus carries food/liquid from the mouth, after swallowing, to the stomach.**

How many teeth are there in the adult human body? **32—including third molars (wisdom teeth).** What are the five senses? **Taste, touch, hearing, sight, and smell.**

Where is the heart located? **Chest or middle.** What does it do? **Circulate or pump blood.**

Where are the lungs located? **Chest or middle.** What do they do? **Breathe or help with breathing.**

The following questions have a more detailed answer for you to share or to use in answering any questions that may arise.

How many bones are there in the skull? Total: 22. **The cranium includes 8: the occipital, two parietals, the frontal, two temporals, the sphenoidal, and the ethmoidal. The facial includes 14: two nasal, two maxillae, two lacrimals, two zygomatics, two palatines, two inferior nasal conchae, the vomer, and the mandible.**

How many bones are there from the knee to the ankle? Total: 2. **The tibia and the fibula.**

How many bones are there from the elbow to the wrist? Total: 2. **The radius and the ulna.**

How many vertebrae are there in the spine? Total: 33. **These include seven cervical (neck), twelve thoracic (mid-back), five lumbar (lower back), five sacrum (fused vertebrae), and four coccyx (the tailbone, also fused vertebrae).**

How many bones are there in one hand? Total: 27. **These include eight carpals (the scaphoid, the lunate, the triquetrium, the pisiform, the trapexium, the trapezoid, the capitate, and the hamate), five metatarsals, and fourteen phalanges.**

How many bones are there in one foot? Total: 26. **These include the talus, the calcaneus, the navicular, the cuboid, three cuneforms (the medial, intermediate, and lateral), five metatarsals, and fourteen phalanges.**

Supply List Price Inventory Form

				Required Supplies			
Item	Package size (dz/lb)	Price of Package	Quantity Purchased	Total Cost	Program Purchase	Employer Furnished	TOTAL PROGRAM COST
							Total A	

		Totals	
	Add Total A:		
	Add Total B:		
	Add Total C:		
	Add Total D:		
	PROGRAM GRAND TOTAL:		

Promotional Supplies							
Item	Package size (dz/lb)	Price of Package	Quantity Purchased	Total Cost	Program Purchase	Employer Furnished	TOTAL PROGRAM COST
						Total B	

Participation Supplies							
Item	Package size (dz/lb)	Price of Package	Quantity Purchased	Total Cost	Program Purchase	Employer Furnished	TOTAL PROGRAM COST
						Total C	

Prize Supplies							
Item	Package size (dz/lb)	Price of Package	Quantity Purchased	Total Cost	Program Purchase	Employer Furnished	TOTAL PROGRAM COST
						Total D	

Quick Reference and Mini Rules Sheet

These rules are very important for maintaining proper safety and to facilitate learning from the program.

- REMEMBER—the program is voluntary. All students or employees do NOT have to participate.
- Take the disability seriously.
- If the involved body part starts to hurt, loses circulation, or experiences pain in any way, remove tape and dispense in garbage.
- If the participant wants to remove the disability before the end of the day, remove tape and dispense in garbage.
- If the participant gets frustrated, remove tape and dispense in garbage.
- The visually-impaired participants require a reliable assistant to guide him/her through school or work facility environment, during lunch time and through certain desk tasks.
- At the end of the day, please return glasses, identifications cards (index cards with disability written on them) and wheelchair to the program therapist before leaving the classroom or work facility. If you had a disability that required tape, please remove tape and dispense in the garbage or place in backpack or work bag to share the experience with family, friends, or coworkers.
- NO switching disabilities after they have been assigned.
- The most important rule of all is to HAVE FUN and LEARN from this experience.
- The wheelchair participants are required to follow the rules above as well as the following:
    - Do not purposely run into people.
    - Do not use the wheelchair as a toy.
    - When using the restroom, you may remove yourself from the wheelchair. If you are interested in trying to transfer yourself from the wheelchair to the toilet, please discuss with the program therapist for transfer technique and transfer with caution. If at any time you feel you may fall or tip over, please remove yourself from the wheelchair immediately and use the restroom as you usually do.
    - When stationary (at desk, in classroom, or in hallway), LOCK BRAKES.
    - Attempt to negotiate the doors of the building. If you require assistance, ask.
    - Other students, school staff, coworkers, or adults may not assist unless asked.

References

American Occupational Therapy Association [AOTA]. (n.d.) Occupational Therapy. Retrieved on March 14, 2006, from the American Occupational Therapy Association Web site: http://www.aota.org/Consumers/WhatisOT.aspx.

Creighton University. (n.d.). Occupational Therapy. Retrieved March 21, 2006, from http://spah0.creighton.edu.

Hole, J.W., Jr. (1993). Human Anatomy & Physiology (6th ed.). Dubuque, IA: Wm. C. Brown Communications, Inc.

Kapit, W. & Elson, L. M. (1977). The Anatomy Coloring Book. New York: Harper & Row.